W9-AZW-477

# THE SCRIPTURAL ROSARY

# THE SCRIPTURAL ROSARY

Edited by
**Rev. Victor Hoagland, C.P.**

Illustrated by
**Blessed Fra Angelico**
(Giovanni da Fiesole)

**Regina**
CLASSICS

**The Regina Press**
New York

*Nihil Obstat:*  Reverend James F. Pereda
                 Censor Delegatus
                 July 16th, 1999

*Imprimatur:*  Most Reverend John R. McGann, D.D
               Bishop of Rockville Center
               July 16th, 1999

# THE SCRIPTURAL ROSARY

## *Mary, the Mother of Jesus*

Mary, the Mother of Jesus, is scarcely mentioned in the gospels; only a few of her words and appearances are recorded in them. Yet she had a key place in the life of her Son.

When the angel Gabriel appeared to her at Nazareth, Mary accepted the invitation to become mother of the Child "who would save his people from their sins." She nursed Jesus as an infant and raised him during the hidden years of Nazareth. When Jesus began his ministry after his baptism in the Jordan, Mary followed him at a distance. Then, when he died on Calvary, she stood beneath the cross and assisted at his burial.

After his resurrection, Mary waited with his other followers for the outpouring of the Holy Spirit at Pentecost. After that, the New Testament hardly mentions her again.

Though scripture scarcely mentions her, Christians over the ages look at Mary as the one closest to Jesus. After all, she was his mother and consented to his birth; she knew him longest in his

lifetime and treasured his memory. Of all Jesus
disciples, Mary knew the Word made flesh most
intimately.

## *A Woman of Faith*

Mary knew her Son, not just by human
experience, but by faith. She was a believer, the
greatest of believers. Like other Jewish women of her
time, she saw life through the lens of the Jewish
scriptures, which were to her God's Word, and she
took their wisdom, their view of history, and their
hope as her own.

Because of her faith, she believed the angel who
announced at Nazareth the mysterious birth of a
Child. Had not the prophets promised a coming
Savior? Had not God told David, " I will raise up your
offspring after you.... and I will establish the throne of
his kingdom forever" (2 Samuel 7:12) God, the
creator of all, the Holy One, was to Mary more
powerful than any creature. She believed the angel's
message, then, and said "Be it done to me according
to your Word."

## *Believing Is Not Seeing*

Believing, however, is not seeing. Mary's world

was hardly ready to welcome a strong new Jewish leader. Roman legions and their allies firmly controlled her land at that time and her people were a captive people. Could anything be done against such mighty armies firmly in control?

She had other questions too. "How can this be, for I do not know a man?" she asked the angel Gabriel at Nazareth. "Why have you done this to us?" she asked her young Son later, when she found him in the temple in Jerusalem after searching for three days. Mary's faith was not naive. She had many questions, and few answers. All her life, God never told her too much; she had to wait and see.

Yet God's will was done. And Mary saw it done, as God's plan unfolded before her eyes at Bethlehem, at Nazareth, and during the events that took place in Jerusalem. As she accompanied Jesus through his life, her faith grew. What she saw made her wonder and praise God.

## *Mary, A Guide for Believers*

Mary, because of her questioning, patient faith, is a good guide for those who wish to know Jesus Christ. In her company, we approach the mysteries of God as she did. Like her, we can discover God's grace hidden as our lives unfold. Her example helps us do God's will day by day. She tells us what she told the stewards at the wedding feast of Cana: "Do what he tells you."

Indeed we never know Jesus on our own. How could we know him, for example, without the great stories of Matthew, Mark, Luke and John, without Paul the Apostle, or Moses or the prophets to tell us about him?

How could we know him without the liturgy of the church, the wisdom of generations of saints, mystics, preachers, theologians, writers, scholars, artists and poets, as well as ordinary Christians?

Yet among these Mary is unique. She knew Jesus from birth to death and resurrection, and she knew him in a special way, as mother. She wrote nothing down, no words, no recollections are directly attributed to her. For the church, however, she is not a writer of recollections. Rather Mary is our fountain of holy wisdom. She is a living guide for believers, the Holy Spirit's agent who helps us understand the mysteries of Christ.

Over the ages, Christians have turned to Mary to fulfill this role. In short, simple words they call upon her and remember her and her Son. A favorite Christian prayer to Mary is the rosary.

## *The Rosary: Where Did It Originate?*

Praying the Rosary well is more important than

knowing its history, yet knowing the origins of the Rosary can teach us much about this great prayer.

The beginnings of the Rosary are found in the early Christian practice of reciting the 150 psalms from the Bible, either daily or weekly. Those unable to recite the psalms began to recite 150 prayers, mainly the Our Father, 150 times, often using beads to count the prayers. By medieval times the custom of saying "Paternoster" beads (Latin, for Our Father) was common throughout Europe. While saying the prayers, it was customary to meditate on the mysteries of the life of Jesus, from his birth to his resurrection.

The present form of the Rosary arose in late medieval Christianity.

## *The Hail Mary*

The Hail Mary evolved as a prayer from the devotion of medieval men and women who saw Mary, the mother to Jesus, as the great witness to his life, death and resurrection. Its earliest form was the greeting made to Mary by the Angel Gabriel:

> *Hail Mary,*
> *full of grace,*
> *the Lord is with you.*                    *Luke 1:28*

Over time the greeting given to Mary by her cousin Elizabeth was added:

*Blessed are you among women*
*and blessed is the fruit of your womb.*

*Luke 1:42*

Finally by the 15th century, the remainder of the prayer appeared:

*Holy Mary, Mother of God,*
*pray for us sinners*
*now and at the hour of our death.*

The prayer calls upon Mary, full of grace and close to her Son, to intercede for us sinners now and at the time our death. We share her as a mother with St. John to whom Jesus entrusted her, when on Calvary he said, "Behold your mother." She will always bring Christ into our life. We trust her to care for us as she cared for the newly married couple at Cana in Galilee. We can go to her in our need.

By the end of the 16th century the practice of saying 150 Hail Marys in series or decades of 10 was popular among many ordinary Christian people. The mysteries of the life, death, and resurrection of Jesus, contained in the Joyful, Sorrowful, and Glorious Mysteries, were remembered during these prayers.

## *Other Prayers of the Rosary*

Other traditional Christian prayers became part of the Rosary such as the Apostles' Creed, an ancient summary of Christian belief. Said in the beginning of the Rosary, it recalls the great truths of faith to us. The Glory Be to the Father, recited at the end of each decade, is an ancient prayer praising the Trinity of Father, Son, and Holy Spirit. Finally, the prayer Hail, Holy Queen came to be recited at the end of the rosary.

## *Mysteries of the Rosary Artwork*
## *by*
## *Blessed Fra Angelico*

Blessed Fra Angelico (Giovanni da Fiesole, 1387-1455), was a friar of the Order of Saint Dominic, the religious community most identified with devotion to the mysteries of the Rosary, both through preaching and through practice. Blessed Fra Angelico added an additional dimension of original creative genius. On the walls of monastic cells, in chapels and churches, as well as in free-standing paintings, Beato Angelico brought to life in his art the Mysteries of the life of Christ and of the life of Mary, his mother. His artwork is prominently featured throughout this book, and enhances the reverence and devotion inherent in the praying of the Scriptural Rosary.

**6.**
Meditate on 3rd Mystery, saying the "Our Father," ten "Hail Marys" and the "Glory Be."

**7.**
Meditate on 4th Mystery, saying the "Our Father," ten "Hail Marys" and the "Glory Be."

**5.**
Meditate on 2nd Mystery, saying the "Our Father," ten "Hail Marys" and the "Glory Be."

**8.**
Meditate on 5th Mystery, saying the "Our Father," ten "Hail Marys and the "Glory Be."

**4.**
Meditate on 1st Mystery, saying the "Our Father," ten "Hail Marys" and the "Glory Be."

**3.**
Say three "Hail Marys" and the "Glory Be."

**2.**
Say the "Our Father".

**9.**
Concluding prayer, "Hail Holy Queen"

**1.**
Make the Sign of the Cross, say the Apostles' Creed.

10

# *How to Say the Rosary*

The complete Rosary consists of fifteen decades, but it is further divided into three distinct parts, the Joyful, the Sorrowful, and the Glorious Mysteries, each containing five decades.

To say the Rosary, begin by making the sign of the cross and saying the Apostles' Creed on the crucifix, one Our Father on the first bead, three Hail Marys on the next three beads, and then a Glory Be to the Father. When this is finished, meditate upon the first mystery, say an Our Father, ten Hail Marys, and one Glory Be to the Father. The first decade is now completed, and to finish the Rosary proceed in the same manner until all five decades have been said.

When this is done, say one Hail Holy Queen.

As a prayer of faith, the Rosary usually begins with two basic summaries of faith: the Sign of the Cross and the Creed. These prayers invite us to believe in God, the Father, the Son, and Holy Spirit, and to remember God's plan of salvation proclaimed in the scriptures.

The Rosary is made up of decades of prayers. A decade of the Rosary consists of an Our Father prayed before ten Hail Marys. At the end of a decade the prayer "Glory be to the Father, and to the Son, and to the Holy Spirit" is said. Most Rosaries have five decades of beads.

## *The Mysteries of the Rosary*

While praying these prayers, you may meditate on the mysteries of Jesus' life and resurrection. Fifteen mysteries are presently associated with the rosary. They are: the Joyful, the Sorrowful, and the Glorious Mysteries.

*The Joyful Mysteries are:*
† The Annunciation
† The Visitation
† The Birth of Jesus
† The Presentation of the Child Jesus in the Temple
† The Finding of the Child Jesus in the Temple

*The Sorrowful Mysteries are:*
† The Agony of Jesus in the Garden
† The Scourging at the Pillar
† The Crowning with Thorns
† The Carrying of the Cross
† The Crucifixion

*The Glorious Mysteries are:*
† The Resurrection of Jesus from the Dead
† The Ascension of Jesus into Heaven
† The Descent of the Holy Spirit
† The Assumption of Mary into Heaven
† The Crowning of Mary Queen of Heaven and Earth

## *Praying the Mysteries on Certain Days*

On certain days associated with a Christian mystery, you may wish to meditate on certain mysteries of the Rosary. For example, Sunday, Wednesday, and Saturday are days associated with the Glorious Mysteries. Tuesdays and Fridays are associated with the Sorrowful Mysteries. Monday and Thursday with the Joyful Mysteries.

During some seasons, such as Lent and Advent, and on certain feasts, you may also wish to remember the mysteries associated with the time or day.

## *Scriptural Verses: Guides to the Mysteries*

To help your meditation on the various mysteries of the Rosary, we offer before each Hail Mary appropriate scripture passages linked to the mystery. When possible, the references are taken from the scriptures of the Old and New Testaments that are read in the church's liturgical celebrations of each mystery during the year. The psalms, which are often used by the Church to summarize a liturgical mystery, make up a major portion of the passages offered.

# Prayers of the Rosary

## The Sign of the Cross

In the name of the Father, ✝ and of the Son, and of the Holy Spirit. Amen.

## The Apostles' Creed

I believe in God, the Father Almighty, Creator of heaven and earth; and in Jesus Christ, his only Son, our Lord, who was conceived by the Holy Spirit; born of the Virgin Mary, suffered under Pontius Pilate, was crucified, died and was buried. He descended into hell; the third day he rose again from the dead; he ascended into heaven, and is seated at the right hand of God the Father; from thence he shall come to judge the living and the dead. I believe in the Holy Spirit, the Holy Catholic Church, the communion of saints, the forgiveness of sins, the resurrection of the body, and life everlasting. Amen.

## The Our Father

Our Father who art in heaven, hallowed be thy name; thy kingdom come; thy will be done on earth as it is in heaven. Give us this day our daily bread; and forgive us our trespasses as we forgive those who trespass against us. And lead us not into temptation; but deliver us from evil. Amen.

## The Hail Mary

Hail Mary, full of grace, the Lord is with you; blessed are you among women, and blessed is the fruit of your womb, Jesus. Holy Mary, Mother of God, pray for us sinners, now and at the hour our death. Amen.

## Glory Be to the Father

Glory be to the Father, and to the Son, and to the Holy Spirit; as it was in the beginning, is now, and ever shall be, world without end. Amen.

## The Hail, Holy Queen

Hail, holy Queen, Mother of Mercy! Our life, our sweetness, and our hope! To thee do we cry, poor banished children of Eve; to thee do we send up our sighs, mourning and weeping in this valley of tears. Turn, then, most gracious advocate, thine eyes of mercy toward us; and after this our exile show unto us the blessed fruit of thy womb Jesus; O clement, O loving, O sweet Virgin Mary.

V. Pray for us, O holy Mother of God.
R. That we may be made worthy of the promises of Christ.

# THE JOYFUL MYSTERIES OF THE ROSARY

Giovanni da Fiesole. *The Annunciation* (1387-1455)

## *The Annunciation*

📖 **Our Father** 📖

Ask a sign of the Lord your God.

*Isaiah 7:11*

✝ **Hail Mary** ✝

Therefore the Lord himself will give you a sign.
Look, the young woman is with child and shall bear
a son, and shall name him Immanuel.

*Isaiah 7:14*

✝ **Hail Mary** ✝

I delight to do your will, O my God...
*Psalm 40:8a*

✝ **Hail Mary** ✝

Your law is within my heart.
*Psalm 40:8b*

✝ **Hail Mary** ✝

I have not concealed your steadfast love and your
faithfulness from the great congregation.
*Psalm 40:10*

✝ **Hail Mary** ✝

But when the fullness of time had come, God sent
his Son, born of a woman,
born under the law.
*Galatians 4:4*

✝ **Hail Mary** ✝

For the Lord has chosen Zion;
he has desired it for his habitation.
*Psalm 132:13*

✝ **Hail Mary** ✝

This is my resting place forever;
here I will reside, for I have desired it.

*Psalm 132:14*

✝ **Hail Mary** ✝

Blessed are you among women, and blessed is the
fruit of your womb.

*Luke 1:42*

✝ **Hail Mary** ✝

My soul magnifies the Lord,
and my spirit rejoices in God my Savior.

*Luke 1:47*

✝ **Hail Mary** ✝

# *The Visitation*

## 📖 Our Father 📖

My soul magnifies the Lord,
and my spirit rejoices in God my Savior.

*Luke 1:47*

## ✝ Hail Mary ✝

For he has looked with favor on
the lowliness of his servant.
Surely, from now on all
generations will call me blessed.

*Luke 1:48*

## ✝ Hail Mary ✝

For the Mighty One has done great things for me,
and holy is his name.

*Luke 1:49*

## ✝ Hail Mary ✝

His mercy is for those who fear him
from generation to generation.

*Luke 1:50*

## ✝ Hail Mary ✝

He has filled the hungry with good things,
and sent the rich away empty.

*Luke 1:53*

✝ Hail Mary ✝

He has helped his servant Israel,
in remembrance of his mercy.

*Luke 1:54*

✝ Hail Mary ✝

Giovanni da Fiesole. *The Visitation* (1387-1455)

My soul longs, indeed it faints
for the courts of the Lord.

*Psalm 84:2a*

✝ **Hail Mary** ✝

My heart and my flesh sing for joy
to the living God.

*Psalm 84:2b*

✝ **Hail Mary** ✝

Even the sparrow finds a home,
and the swallow a nest for herself,
where she may lay her young,
at your altars, O Lord of hosts,
my King and my God.

*Psalm 84:3*

✝ **Hail Mary** ✝

For a day in your courts is better
than a thousand elsewhere.

*Psalm 84:10*

✝ **Hail Mary** ✝

Giovanni da Fiesole. *The Birth of Jesus* (1387-1455)

## *The Birth of Jesus*

📖 **Our Father** 📖

Say to daughter Zion,
"See, your salvation comes,
his reward is with him,
and his recompense before him."

*Isaiah 62:11*

✝ **Hail Mary** ✝

How beautiful upon the mountains
are the feet of the messenger
who announces peace, who brings good news,
who announces salvation,
who says to Zion, "Your God reigns."

*Isaiah 52:7*

✝ **Hail Mary** ✝


Break forth together into singing,
you ruins of Jerusalem;
for the Lord has comforted his people,
he has redeemed Jerusalem.

*Isaiah 52:9*

✝ **Hail Mary** ✝


For the grace of God has appeared,
bringing salvation to all.

*Titus 2:11*

✝ **Hail Mary** ✝


Rejoice in the Lord, O you righteous,
and give thanks to his holy name!

*Psalm 97:12*

✝ **Hail Mary** ✝

Long ago God spoke to our ancestors in
many and various ways by the prophets, but in
these last days he has spoken to us by a Son.
*Hebrews 1:1, 2*

✝ **Hail Mary** ✝

In the beginning was the Word, and the Word was
with God, and the Word was God.
*John 1:1*

✝ **Hail Mary** ✝

And the Word became flesh and lived among us,
and we have seen his glory, the glory as of a father's
only son, full of grace and truth.
*John 1:14*

✝ **Hail Mary** ✝

From his fullness we have all received,
grace upon grace.
*John 1:16*

✝ **Hail Mary** ✝

No one has ever seen God.
It is God the only Son,
who is close to the Father's heart,
who has made him known.
*John 1:18*

✝ **Hail Mary** ✝

Giovanni da Fiesole. *The Presentation of the Child Jesus in the Temple* (1387-1455)

## *The Presentation of the Child Jesus in the Temple*

📖 Our Father 📖

When the time came for their
purification according to the law of Moses,
they brought him up to Jerusalem
to present him to the Lord.

*Luke 2:22*

✝ Hail Mary ✝

See, I am sending my messenger
to prepare the way before me....

*Malachi 3:1a*

✝ Hail Mary ✝

And the Lord whom you seek
will suddenly come to his temple.

*Malachi 3:1b*


✝ Hail Mary ✝


The messenger of the covenant in whom you
delight - indeed, he is coming,
says the Lord of hosts.

*Malachi 3:1c*


✝ Hail Mary ✝


Lift up your heads, O gates!
and be lifted up, O ancient doors!
that the King of glory may come in.

*Psalm 24:7*


✝ Hail Mary ✝


Who is the King of glory?
The Lord, strong and mighty,
the Lord, mighty in battle.

*Psalm 24:8*


✝ Hail Mary ✝

Who is this King of glory?
The Lord of hosts,
he is the King of glory.

*Psalm 24:10*

✝ **Hail Mary** ✝

Master, now you are dismissing
your servant in peace,
according to your word...

*Luke 2:29*

✝ **Hail Mary** ✝

For my eyes have seen your salvation,
which you have prepared in the
presence of all peoples.

*Luke 2:30*

✝ **Hail Mary** ✝

A light for revelation to the Gentiles
and for glory to your people Israel.

*Luke 2:32*

✝ **Hail Mary** ✝

# *The Finding of the Child Jesus in the Temple*

## 📖 Our Father 📖

When they did not find him, they returned to
Jerusalem to search for him.
*Luke 2:45*

## ✝ Hail Mary ✝

After three days they found him in the temple,
sitting among the teachers, listening to them
and asking questions.
*Luke 2:46*

## ✝ Hail Mary ✝

Giovanni da Fiesole. *The Finding of the Child Jesus
in the Temple* (1387-1455)

Then he went down with them and came to
Nazareth, and was obedient to them.

*Luke 2:51*

✝ **Hail Mary** ✝

And Jesus increased in wisdom and in years, and in
divine and human favor.

*Luke 2:52*

✝ **Hail Mary** ✝

Happy is everyone who fears the Lord,
who walks in his ways.

*Psalm 128:1*

✝ **Hail Mary** ✝

For the Lord honors a father above his children,
and he confirms a mother's right
over her children.

*Sirach 3:2*

✝ **Hail Mary** ✝

Teach and admonish one another in all wisdom.

*Colossians 3:16*

✝ **Hail Mary** ✝

And let the peace of Christ rule in your hearts,
to which indeed you were
called in the one body...
*Colossians 3:15a*

✝ **Hail Mary** ✝

And be thankful.
*Colossians 3:15b*

✝ **Hail Mary** ✝

Let the word of Christ dwell in you richly.
*Colossians 3:16*

✝ **Hail Mary** ✝

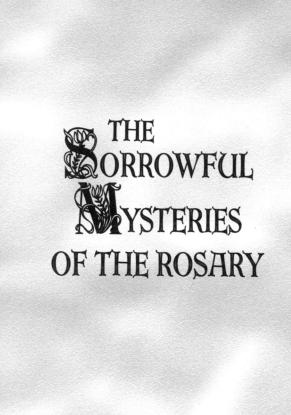

# THE SORROWFUL MYSTERIES OF THE ROSARY

### *The Agony of Jesus in the Garden*

📖 Our Father 📖

In the days of his flesh,
Jesus offered up prayers and supplications,
with loud cries and tears,
to the one who was able to
save him from death...

*Hebrew 5:7a*

✝ Hail Mary ✝

And he was heard because of his reverent
submission.

*Hebrew 5:7b*

✝ Hail Mary ✝

Although he was a Son, he learned obedience
through what he suffered.

*Hebrew 5:8*

✝ Hail Mary ✝

I have become a stranger to my kindred,
an alien to my mother's children.

*Psalm 69:8*

✝ Hail Mary ✝

It is zeal for your house that has consumed me;
the insults of those who insult
you have fallen on me.

*Psalm 69:9*

✝ **Hail Mary** ✝

With your faithful help rescue me
from sinking in the mire...

*Psalm 69:13a*

✝ **Hail Mary** ✝

Let me be delivered from my enemies
and from the deep waters.

*Psalm 69:13b*

✝ **Hail Mary** ✝

Answer me, O Lord, for your
steadfast love is good;
according to your abundant mercy, turn to me.

*Psalm 69:16*

✝ **Hail Mary** ✝

Do not hide your face from your servant,
for I am in distress - make haste to answer me.
*Psalm 69:17*

✝ Hail Mary ✝

For the Lord hears the needy,
and does not despise his own that are in bonds.
*Psalm 69:33*

✝ Hail Mary ✝

Giovanni da Fiesole. *The Agony of Jesus in the Garden* (1387-1455)

## *The Scourging at the Pillar*

### 📖 Our Father 📖

Why are your robes red,
and your garments like theirs
who tread the wine press?
*Isaiah 63:2*

### ✝ Hail Mary ✝

I have trodden the wine press alone,
and from the peoples no one was with me.
*Isaiah 63:3*

### ✝ Hail Mary ✝

I looked, but there was no helper;
I stared, but there was no one to sustain me.
*Isaiah 63:5*

### ✝ Hail Mary ✝

I will recount the gracious deeds of the Lord,
the praiseworthy acts of the Lord.
*Isaiah 63:7*

### ✝ Hail Mary ✝

All who see me mock at me;
they make mouths at me, they
shake their heads.

*Psalm 22:7*

✝ **Hail Mary** ✝

For dogs are all around me;
a company of evil doers encircles me.

*Psalm 22:16*

✝ **Hail Mary** ✝

They divide my clothes
among themselves,
and for my clothing they cast lots.

*Psalm 22:18*

✝ **Hail Mary** ✝

But you, O Lord, do not be far away!

*Psalm 22:19a*

✝ **Hail Mary** ✝

O my help, come quickly to my aid!

*Psalm 22:19b*

✝ **Hail Mary** ✝

I will tell of your name
to my brothers and sisters;
in the midst of the congregation
I will praise you.

*Psalm 22:22*

✝ **Hail Mary** ✝

Giovanni da Fiesole. *The Scourging at the Pillar* (1387-1455)

# *The Crowning with Thorns*

## 📖 Our Father 📖

Who has believed what we have heard?
*Isaiah 53:1*

### ✝ Hail Mary ✝

He had no form or majesty that
we should look at him,
nothing in his appearance that
we should desire him.
*Isaiah 53:2*

### ✝ Hail Mary ✝

He was despised and rejected by others;
a man of suffering and
acquainted with infirmity.
*Isaiah 53:3*

### ✝ Hail Mary ✝

Surely he has borne our infirmities
and carried our diseases;
yet we accounted him stricken,
struck down by God, and afflicted.
*Isaiah 53:4*

### ✝ Hail Mary ✝

But he was wounded for our transgressions,
crushed for our iniquities.

*Isaiah 53:5*

✝ **Hail Mary** ✝

Giovanni da Fiesole. *The Crowning with Thorns* (1387-1455)

He was oppressed, and he was afflicted,
yet he did not open his mouth...

*Isaiah 53:7a*

† **Hail Mary** †


Like a lamb that is led to the slaughter,
and like a sheep that before its shearers is silent,
so he did not open his mouth.

*Isaiah 53:7b*

† **Hail Mary** †


It is for your sake that I have borne reproach,
that shame has covered my face.

*Psalm 69:7*

† **Hail Mary** †


Insults have broken my heart,
so that I am in despair.

*Psalm 69:20a*

† **Hail Mary** †


I looked for pity, but there was none;
and for comforters, but I found none.

*Psalm 69:20b*

† **Hail Mary** †

### *The Carrying of the Cross*

📖 Our Father 📖

I gave my back to those who struck me,
and my cheeks to those
who pulled out the beard...
*Isaiah 50:6a*

✝ Hail Mary ✝

I did not hide my face from insult and spitting.
*Isaiah 50:6b*

✝ Hail Mary ✝

Giovanni da Fiesole. *The Carrying of the Cross* (1387-1455)

The Lord God helps me...
*Isaiah 50:7a*

✝ **Hail Mary** ✝

Therefore I have set my face like flint,
and I know that I shall not be put to shame.
*Isaiah 50:7b*

✝ **Hail Mary** ✝

[Jesus Christ] emptied himself,
taking the form of a slave,
being born in human likeness...
*Philippians 2:7*

✝ **Hail Mary** ✝

And being found in human form,
he humbled himself
and became obedient to the point of death -
even death on a cross.
*Philippians 2:8*

✝ **Hail Mary** ✝

Therefore God also highly exalted him
and gave him the name
that is above every name.

*Philippians 2:9*

✝ Hail Mary ✝

So that at the name of Jesus
every knee should bend...

*Philippians 2:10*

✝ Hail Mary ✝

And every tongue should confess
that Jesus Christ is Lord,
to the glory of God the Father.

*Philippians 2:11*

✝ Hail Mary ✝

Let the same mind be in you that
was in Christ Jesus.

*Philippians 2:5*

✝ Hail Mary ✝

# *The Crucifixion*

## 📖 Our Father 📖

In you, O Lord, I seek refuge;
do not let me ever be put to shame;
in your righteousness deliver me.
*Psalm 31:1*

## ✝ Hail Mary ✝

Into your hand I commit my spirit...
*Psalm 31:5a*

## ✝ Hail Mary ✝

You have redeemed me,
O Lord, faithful God.
*Psalm 31:5b*

## ✝ Hail Mary ✝

I am the scorn of all my adversaries,
a horror to my neighbors,
an object of dread to my acquaintances;
those who see me in the street flee from me.
*Psalm 31:11*

## ✝ Hail Mary ✝

Giovanni da Fiesole. *The Crucifixion* (1387-1455)

I have passed out of mind like one who is dead;
I have become like a broken vessel.

*Psalm 31:12*

✝ Hail Mary ✝

But I trust in you, O Lord;
I say, "You are my God."

*Psalm 31:14*

✝ Hail Mary ✝

My times are in your hand;
deliver me from from the hand of my enemies and
persecutors.

*Psalm 31:15*

✝ Hail Mary ✝

Let your face shine upon your servant;
save me in your steadfast love.

*Psalm 31:16*

✝ Hail Mary ✝

Be strong, and let your heart take courage,
all you who wait for the Lord.

*Psalm 31:24*

✝ Hail Mary ✝

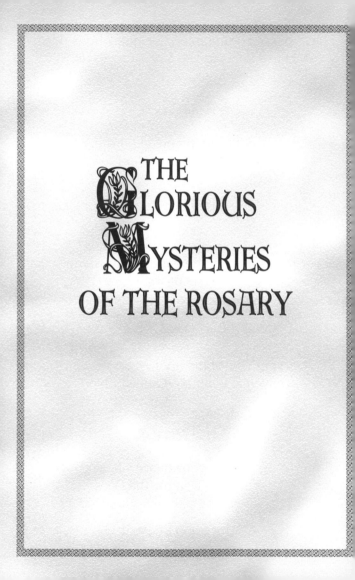

# THE GLORIOUS MYSTERIES OF THE ROSARY

Giovanni da Fiesole. *The Resurrection of Jesus from the Dead* (1387-1455)

## *The Resurrection of Jesus from the Dead*

📖 **Our Father** 📖

But God raised him on the third day
and allowed him to appear...
*Acts 10:40*

✝ **Hail Mary** ✝

Not to all the people but to us who
were chosen by God as witnesses,
and who ate and drank with him
after he rose from the dead.

*Acts 10:41*

✝ Hail Mary ✝

So if you have been raised with Christ,
seek the things that are above,
where Christ is,
seated at the right hand of God.

*Colossians 3:1*

✝ Hail Mary ✝

This is the day the Lord has made;
let us rejoice and be glad in it.

*Psalm 118:24*

✝ Hail Mary ✝

O give thanks to the Lord, for he is good,
for his steadfast love endures forever.

*Psalm 118:29*

✝ Hail Mary ✝

I shall not die, but I shall live,
and recount the deeds of the Lord.
*Psalm 118:17*

✝ **Hail Mary** ✝

The stone that the builders rejected has become
the chief cornerstone.
*Psalm 118:22*

✝ **Hail Mary** ✝

This is the Lord's doing;
it is marvelous in our eyes.
*Psalm 118:23*

✝ **Hail Mary** ✝

Giovanni da Fiesole. *The Ascension of Jesus into Heaven* (1387-1455)

## *The Ascension of Jesus into Heaven*

### 📖 Our Father 📖

After his suffering he presented himself alive to
them by many convincing proofs...

*Acts 1:3a*

### ✝ Hail Mary ✝

...appearing to them during forty days and speaking
about the kingdom of God.

*Acts 1:3b*

### ✝ Hail Mary ✝

He was lifted up,
and a cloud took him out of their sight.

*Acts 1:9*

### ✝ Hail Mary ✝

So that, with the eyes of your heart enlightened,
you may know what is the
hope to which he has called you.

*Ephesians 1:18*

### ✝ Hail Mary ✝

Clap your hands, all you peoples;
shout to God with loud songs of joy.
*Psalm 47:1*

**✝ Hail Mary ✝**

For the Lord, the Most High, is awesome,
a great king over all the earth.
*Psalm 47:2*

**✝ Hail Mary ✝**

God has gone up with a shout,
the Lord with the sound of a trumpet.
*Psalm 47:5*

**✝ Hail Mary ✝**

God is king over the nations;
God sits on his holy throne.
*Psalm 47:8*

**✝ Hail Mary ✝**

Go therefore and make disciples of all nations,
baptizing them in the name of the Father and of the
Son and of the Holy Spirit.

*Matthew 28:19*

✝ **Hail Mary** ✝

And remember, I am with you always,
to the end of the age.

*Matthew 28:20*

✝ **Hail Mary** ✝

# *The Descent of the Holy Spirit*

### 📖 Our Father 📖

Then afterward
I will pour out my spirit on all flesh...
*Joel 2:28a*

### ✝ Hail Mary ✝

Your sons and your daughters shall prophesy...
*Joel 2:28b*

### ✝ Hail Mary ✝

Your old men shall dream dreams...
*Joel 2:28c*

### ✝ Hail Mary ✝

And your young men shall see visions.
*Joel 2:28d*

### ✝ Hail Mary ✝

Likewise the Spirit helps us in our weakness; for we
do not know how to pray as we ought...
*Romans 8:26a*

### ✝ Hail Mary ✝

But that very Spirit intercedes
with sighs too deep for words.
*Romans 8:26b*

✝ Hail Mary ✝

Giovanni da Fiesole. *The Descent of the Holy Spirit* (1387-1455)

Bless the Lord, O my soul.
O Lord my God, you are very great.
*Psalm 104:1*

✝ **Hail Mary** ✝

These all look to you
to give them their food in due season;
*Psalm 104:27*

✝ **Hail Mary** ✝

When you give to them, they gather it up;
when you open your hand,
they are filled with good things.
*Psalm 104:28*

✝ **Hail Mary** ✝

When you send forth your spirit,
they are created;
and you renew the face of the ground.
*Psalm 104:30*

✝ **Hail Mary** ✝

# *The Assumption of Mary into Heaven*

📖 Our Father 📖

The man named his wife Eve,
because she was the mother of all living.
*Genesis 3:20*

✝ Hail Mary ✝

O sing to the Lord a new song.
*Psalm 98:1*

✝ Hail Mary ✝

The Lord has made known his victory;
he has revealed his vindication
in the sight of the nations.
*Psalm 98:2*

✝ Hail Mary ✝

He has remembered his steadfast
love and faithfulness
to the house of Israel.
*Psalm 98:3a*

✝ Hail Mary ✝

All the ends of the earth have seen
the victory of our God.

*Psalm 98:3b*

✝ **Hail Mary** ✝

Make a joyful noise to the Lord,
all the earth...

*Psalm 98:4c*

✝ **Hail Mary** ✝

Break forth into joyous song and sing praises.

*Psalm 98:4b*

✝ **Hail Mary** ✝

Blessed be the God and Father of our Lord Jesus
Christ, who has blessed us in Christ with every
spiritual blessing in the heavenly places.

*Ephesians 1:3*

✝ **Hail Mary** ✝

Just as he chose us in Christ
before the foundation of the world
to be holy and blameless before him in love.

*Ephesians 1:4*

✝ **Hail Mary** ✝

Giovanni da Fiesole. *The Assumption of Mary into Heaven* (1387-1455)

## *The Crowning of Mary Queen of Heaven and Earth*

### 📖 Our Father 📖

For a child has been born for us,
a son given to us;
authority rests upon his shoulders.
*Isaiah 9:6a*

### ✝ Hail Mary ✝

And he is named
Wonderful Counselor, Mighty God,
Everlasting Father, Prince of Peace.
*Isaiah 9:6b*

### ✝ Hail Mary ✝

Hear, O daughter,
consider and incline your ear;
forget your people
and your father's house,
and the king will desire your beauty.
*Psalm 45:10*

### ✝ Hail Mary ✝

The princess is decked in her chamber
with gold-woven robes...

*Psalm 45:14a*

✝ **Hail Mary** ✝


In many-colored robes
she is led to the king;
behind her the virgins,
her companions, follow...

*Psalm 45:14b*

✝ **Hail Mary** ✝


With joy and gladness
they are led along
as they enter the
palace of the king.

Psalm 45:15

✝ **Hail Mary** ✝


I will cause your name to be
celebrated in all generations;
therefore the peoples will praise
you forever and ever.

*Psalm 45:17*

✝ **Hail Mary** ✝

Giovanni da Fiesole. *The Crowning of Mary Queen of Heaven and Earth* (1387-1455)

O daughter, you are blessed by the Most High God
above all other women on earth.

*Judith 13:18*

**✝ Hail Mary ✝**

Your praise will never depart from the hearts of
those who remember the power of God.

*Judith 13:19*

**✝ Hail Mary ✝**

Giovanni da Fiesole. *Madonna and Child* (1387-1455)

# *Litany of the Blessed Virgin Mary*

Lord, have mercy,
Christ, have mercy,
Lord, have mercy.
Christ, hear us.
Christ, graciously hear us.
God, the Father of heaven, have mercy on us.
God, the Son, Redeemer of the world,
    have mercy on us.
God, the Holy Spirit, have mercy on us.
Holy Trinity, one God, have mercy on us.
Holy Mary,
(after each invocation, respond with,
    "Pray for us")
                              -Pray for us.
Holy Mother of God,
Holy Virgin of virgins,
Mother of Christ,
Mother, full of grace,
Mother most pure,
Mother most chaste,
Immaculate Mother,
Sinless Mother,
Lovable Mother,

Model of mothers,
Mother of good counsel,
Mother of our Maker,
Mother of our Savior,
Wisest of virgins,
Holiest of virgins,
Virgin, powerful in the sight of God,
Virgin, merciful to us sinners,
Virgin, faithful to all God asks of you,
Mirror of holiness,
Seat of wisdom,
Cause of our joy,
Shrine of the Spirit,
Honor of your people,
Devoted handmaid of the Lord,
Mystical Rose,
Tower of David,
Tower of ivory,
House of gold,
Ark of the covenant,
Gate of heaven,
Star of hope,
Health of the sick,
Refuge of sinners,
Comfort of the afflicted,

Help of Christians,
Queen of angels,
Queen of patriarchs,
Queen of prophets,
Queen of apostles,
Queen of martyrs,
Queen of confessors,
Queen of virgins,
Queen of all saints,
Queen conceived in holiness,
Queen raised up to glory,
Queen of the Rosary,
Queen of peace,
Lamb of God, you take away the sins
     of the world,   – Spare us, O Lord.
Lamb of God, you take away the sins
     of the world,
          – Graciously hear us, O Lord.
Lamb of God, you take away the sins
     of the world,  – Have mercy on us.

Pray for us, O holy Mother of God,
        – That we may be made worthy
             of the promises of Christ.
Let us pray.

Lord God,
   give to your people the joy of
   continual health in mind and body.

With the prayers of the Virgin Mary
   to help us, guide us through
   the sorrows of this life to
   eternal happiness in the life to come.

We ask this through Christ our Lord.   Amen.